An Outrageous Idea:

Natural Prayer

An Outrageous Idea:
Natural Prayer

Patty Jo Cornish
Illustrations by James Hubbell

Hilltop House Publishers, Inc.
San Diego, California

An Outrageous Idea – Natural Prayer
Copyright © 1996 by Patty Jo Cornish
All rights reserved.

No part of this book may be used or
reproduced in any manner without
written permission except in the case
of brief quotations embodied in critical
articles and reviews.
For information address Hilltop House Publishers, Inc.,
P.O. Box 90928, San Diego, CA 92169

Printed in the United States of America
First Edition

**With special thanks to Mike Marcon
for his prodding, mentoring, and copywriting**

**James Hubbell, Illustrator
Erin Garth, book designer and angel
Nancy Gillan, Michelangelo of copy editors**

Library of Congress Number Preassigned 95-094862
ISBN 09613717-1-4

To all children everywhere
including the adult ones,
who have a right to know about
and choose, *if they wish,*
the *possibilities*
of their Higher Selves
and the joy, freedom and
spiritual power
of **Natural Prayer.**

An Outrageous Idea
Natural Prayer

≈

We need a miracle. We have forgotten that we are all in this together. And we keep separating ourselves from ourselves, by color, by football teams, by clothes, by money, by creed, by greed, by boundaries, by age, and so on and on. We need something that will pull us all together. *Natural Prayer* could be that something, that miracle. It includes everyone, even the nonbelievers.

THE STANFORD STORY

A few summers ago I was sitting on a peaceful green lawn at Stanford University with a group of enthusiastic and very bright young people. They were high-school and college elected leaders. We were there as part of a California Association of Student Councils (CASC) leadership training conference. Directed by Dr. June Thompson, it offered outstanding training, utilizing the best of current leadership and management techniques; and these young people were learning rapidly. The college-age students were leading much of the conference, and it was amazing to witness their efficiency and their effectiveness in achieving group goals. If our country is not too messed up by the time these young people are in leadership positions, they might show us all how to pull together, as they had been doing throughout the conference in work and play periods. Everyone was included in every activity, and they were having fun and learning.

I felt privileged to be one of their instructors and even more privileged to be included in this impromptu rap session. I was quietly listening to them and being amazed. In a group which included a diversity of color and culture, they were telling and asking each other about their life missions.

"Do you know your life mission?" they asked.

Some seemed very certain of their missions, others had possible ideas, and a few merely sat pondering the new thoughts they were hearing. Meanwhile, I listened and was elated that young people in this time and day had the idea that each had a mission to accomplish in her or his lifetime, and that they were all actively thinking about it.

I hadn't even heard of a "life mission" until my late forties. Since then, with much resistance, I had come to know my own mission; I now feel that everyone has a life purpose of joy as well as service. Each mission is equally important. It may be as simple as being kind to people or as complicated as being a President!

Of course, one student finally turned to me and asked, "Patty Jo, do you know your life mission?"

Slowly and somewhat reluctantly I replied, "Yes, I do." I hesitated to share because I knew my mission all too well, and it had been "on hold" for what I knew was too long. I was living it but not speaking about it unless directly asked. And, in the instant that the student asked me the question, I reminded myself that young people have a way of knowing intuitively whether adults are being real about who they are. I knew I was going to have to tell them my truth, risking that they might not understand or worse, that they might understand and disagree strongly. My mission then, as it does now, concerns a highly controversial subject, a subject most people don't even want to talk about. Some become angry just hearing the key word.

By now they were all clamoring, "What is it, what is it?"

"Well," I replied, "I can explain it to you more easily if you will imagine that I am one of your high-school teachers and you are coming into my class which is about to begin. You know what it's like when you are entering class, lots of activity, high spirits, some low spirits, and much movement. And, I say to you as you come in, "Listen, gang, before we begin our class work, let's take a couple of deep breaths, and for a few moments, let's go inside ourselves quietly and find our best self—you know, the self that stays focused and learns the easiest?

"Maybe your girlfriend just turned you down, or you flunked last period's test, or your mom yelled at you as you left this morning. Actually, I'm a little distracted because my car was acting strangely this morning. Let's simply let all those things go for this period and find our highest selves. One reason for doing that is that the hour will go faster and we will learn much more easily.

"Now if you call that prayer, that's okay. If you call it meditation, that's okay too. If you don't want to do either of those things and just want to enjoy the quiet, or sleep for the next few minutes, that's also okay. We promise we won't disturb you. So, relax, take some deep breaths and..."

Before I finished, the students were already responding, exclaiming, "Oh, wouldn't it be great if a class could begin like that!" Or they were saying to each other, "It would be wonderful, and everyone would participate!"

And then bewilderment surfaced among them. "Why don't teachers do that?"

I paused, then slowly answered, "Let me tell you something. If I said that to you exactly as I just said it, I would be breaking the law three different ways." They were astounded. They knew they weren't supposed to be religious at school, but this scene seemed so right, even healthy! "Well, here is what's wrong with what I did. I told you it was okay to pray; I told you it was okay to meditate; and I allowed class time to do that." I looked around at the group. Their faces were full of surprise, some were crestfallen, some even angry. They expressed dismay and outrage at the unfairness.

Things haven't changed much since then. Chaos swirls around the ruling about prayer in schools; while it may now be all right to have a moment of silence and/or meditation, even that has been challenged, leaving teachers confused and sometimes even afraid. And it is definitely illegal for a teacher to say its okay to pray in the classroom, or say it is all right to pray silently, or allow time specifically for prayer or meditation.

Strangely, however, prayer has never been outlawed on the playing field. It was always okay, even encouraged, to seek a higher source, the Spirit that binds us and the team together! Spirit is evoked on the playing field, with cheerleaders to build it. Everyone knows that if we are all together in Spirit, our team will do better! And, of course, after professional *and* school touchdowns all over the country there have been prayers. Isn't that interesting?

My concluding statement to the group of students was, "So my mission is about restoring the recognition of Spirit to the classroom by showing that there are basically two kinds of prayer; religious prayer, which is what the constitutional amendment is about, and nonreligious prayer, which is what we all do ***naturally***—, consciously, unconsciously, or in disguise!"

Since that very special afternoon I have often remembered and been inspired by those students and their reactions. I knew then that I had to do more than simply live my mission, I had to act on it with conviction. The ideas in this little book were first written over ten years ago. I did not fully realize it then, but I had taken the first step of many that have led to my understanding that nonreligious prayer is truly a natural act, and we can call it *Natural Prayer.*

The remainder of this book contains new and outrageous ways to look at something simple that we have made complicated. In the process of making it complicated, and complex, we have separated ourselves in a time when more than ever we need to exist in harmony. Please read slowly, with an open mind, and then draw your conclusions.

In love and Spirit,

Patty Jo Cornish

This is a primer about prayer, and a "primer" is a book that starts at the beginning. The reason we need a primer about prayer is that for thousands of years we have been making it complicated. We have added words and forms and symbols and rituals and body postures. And then we added more words and something called theology.

Somehow, what prayer is all about got lost. We began to believe that it was about words—very specific words—like "religious," "church," "Dear Jesus," "Oh God," and "Amen." We also began to believe that we were supposed to go to a church or a temple or a synagogue or a mosque to learn about prayer. Nowadays, some people in the United States think that prayer can be defined by the Constitution; that it can be understood by talking about the separation of Church and State. We seem to have made it all very complicated.

So, what is prayer exactly?

To clear it all up we may need to get back to a time when a human being first prayed and ask him *why* he did that and *how* he did that and *what* was the result.

In the process, maybe we can write a primer together about prayer. Primers state information very simply and sometimes there are stories and pictures to help make the subject clear. Maybe, as we do this together, we will wind up back at the beginning.

Perhaps the lessons we put first in the primer could temporarily set aside some things, like:

1

Prayer is not a religious act.

Maybe you'll want to copy that statement yourself to see what it might mean to you. Maybe you think it is an outrageous idea. *You don't have to believe it to think about it.*

2

Prayer is not dangerous separated from church.

If that lesson is true, then prayer could come out of the churches and temples and see the sunshine. And some people think that could be dangerous.

These first two lessons are about what prayer *isn't*. That's because when something is tightly connected to something else, we can't get a clear picture of how it looks and what it does by itself. So we need to separate prayer from religion and from church to see if it can stand alone.

When we think of how prayer might first have happened, there doesn't seem to be anything called churches or temples yet. There doesn't seem to be anything called "religion" either.

Maybe, then, our third lesson is:

3

Prayer happened before
religion happened.

Could it have happened something like this:

A Simple Story

One day a long time ago, a young man roamed the plains in search of food. He was very hungry. He hadn't eaten anything for many, many days. He had looked in all the places he had found food before and still had found none. As he became weaker from lack of food, his steps became slower and slower.

Soon he stumbled and fell. Struggling, he found he was too weak to pull himself up. In despair he lay, believing that soon he would die . He had used up all the information in his head about finding food and still had found no food. He reasoned that since he had used all his information without success, there must be no food left anywhere in his world.

Quietly, lying on his back looking up at the sky, he suddenly had a new thought: Is there something I *do not* know? Could there be something greater than I that *does* know?

With a burst of energy from the promising thought, he flung his arms wide and called out to the sky, "Do you know what I do not? Do you know where there is food that I may have so I will not starve?"

As the back of his hand touched the ground, he felt a hard lump. Quickly digging with his hands he discovered, to his great delight, a thick root! After brushing the dirt from the root, he gratefully and loudly devoured the root. Discovering more roots buried nearby, he soon ate his fill.

Resting from the excitement, he once again lay back and looked up at the sky. In awe, he wondered about the event that had just passed.

The sky has more power and knows things that I do not, he reasoned, and soon he was sure of it. He believed the sky had saved him from starvation and shown him where there was food *because he had asked.* Humbly, and with astonishment, he again flung his arms wide and thanked the sky, which he now called "Oh Sky."

If we make this the end of our primer's first chapter, we can discuss what has happened so far.

Did Sky cause him to find food? Could we ever know for sure? Is it important to know for sure? (Is it okay for primers to ask questions instead of giving all answers?) A famous man named Rainer Maria Rilke once said, "Live your questions now, and perhaps, without even knowing it, you will live along some distant day into your answers." So, let's ask the questions and maybe we will have the answers by the end of our primer.

Maybe the only thing that is important is that the young man in our story *asked* for help from outside himself. The *asking* had given him new strength to move, and the moving had resulted in his finding food. He seemed to have found food from the *act* of *seeking a power higher than himself.*

Isn't this reminiscent of a Bible verse that goes, "Ask, and you will receive; seek and you will find; knock, and the door will be opened to you?"

Maybe an answer to our question, "What is prayer, exactly?" can be lesson number four. Let's try it out:

4

Prayer is simple acknowledgement of a power higher than the one praying.

"Simple acknowledgement" could mean crying out loudly, or quietly, like "Oh Sky."

If that lesson is true, then religions and special buildings do not seem to be necessary or required for a person to pray.

The Second Chapter of the Simple Story

With his energy regained, and an armful of roots, the young man found his way back to his people and excitedly told them the story of what had happened to him. He told them about Sky, and when he said the word he said it reverently. He told them exactly how he was lying on the ground with his arms outstretched when Sky gave him what he had asked for.

He told them he *believed* Sky had answered his seeking, his prayer. He taught them to believe in Sky and how to lie on their backs with their arms outstretched to pray to Sky. He traveled all over the land to tell people about Sky. Then he began to teach the children about

Sky and showed them how to pray to Sky. Some of the children wondered why they should seek Sky when he had already been found.

Soon people were writing about Sky, and a building had been built in his honor. The building was used to teach about Sky and how to pray to Sky. After a time, the people began to believe that the only place to find Sky was in the building. So the building became very important. It was called the Temple of Sky.

Let's end Chapter Two here and discuss the story some more.

Now it appears we have a *religion* started. Religions seem to be sets of words, symbols, and rituals that explain a higher power. It also appears that people had to invent religion so that they could talk to each other about their experiences in seeking a higher power. How could they talk without using *words?* And it does seem much easier to teach about things when we can use *words* most people agree with and understand. The trouble with *words* is that people begin to think that the *words* are the real thing. They forget what the *words* stand for, and that the original *words* were simply chosen by human beings.

Anyway, it does seem that *prayer happened before religion happened,* doesn't it?

Now, it seems safe to suggest a fifth lesson from this deduction:

5

The way you pray
may be a religious act.

If you use somebody else's words and position and ritual, that starts to sound very religious, doesn't it?

Well, it appears as if it's time to ask the really big question. If we are sincere with this learning primer, we must be brave and ask all of the questions that come up. This one has already appeared more than once.

Does a Higher Power Exist?

DOES A HIGHER POWER REALLY EXIST?

How can we know? *If* knowing means having facts with which something can be proven here on Earth, and the higher power extends beyond Earth (it certainly seems that if we are going to believe in a higher power, it had better *not* be Earthbound), how in Earth language can we *know* it or *not* know it?

Using that reasoning then, we should be able to safely add these lessons to our primer:

6

We cannot know
that a higher power exists.

7

We cannot know
that a higher power
does not exist.

We all know people who seem to "know" some things without words to explain them. "Knowing" like that is sometimes described as "right-brained"—and sometimes it is called *faith*. If we agree that the higher power is beyond Earth and cannot be explained with our finite *words*, then maybe our right brain is our connection *outside* Earth space.

To end any confusion we might have, maybe information is available that will help us decide for ourselves, *inside* ourselves and *all by ourselves*. But it certainly would be easier to find someone else to simply tell us all the answers, wouldn't it?

Maybe the following scientific words on the matter will help:

8

The whole is greater than the sum of the parts.

Earlier in this century, scientists argued about that; but recent work in quantum physics seems to prove that it is true. It may mean, for instance, that when people combine their energy, they create something greater than simply the combining of each person's energy.

9

Everything is connected to everything else.

All scientists seem to agree with this lesson. It is the reason environmentalists get so excited about every little thing. They believe that *anything* we do with our environment affects *everything* in our environment.

Now some scientists take these lessons a step further and believe that, ultimately, we are all one thing. Think about that for a minute...

Maybe that is what some religious groups mean when they say we are each a part of the higher power, whatever name they have for it.

The trouble with looking to scientists for final answers is that in nearly every branch of science there are groups who disagree on the possible answers.

So it still seems as if, in the end, we have to seek our answers for ourselves. We can't wait around for all those scientists to agree with each other.

Could it be that the "whole" that is greater than the sum of the parts *is* that higher power? And *if* everything is connected, and we are a part of that connection...

could it be that *prayer*, the simple acknowledgement of a higher power, is the method we could use to make that connection?

While we think about that, let's get back to our story.

Sometimes an idea needs time to run through all the programs in our heads to see if it fits comfortably with everything else in there. When it does, sometimes we get an "Aha!" But not all "Ahas" come instantly.

Now, before we begin writing the next chapter, please consider this lesson: (Remember the old saying, "Sticks and stones may break my bones, but words can never harm me"? Well . . .)

10

Words *can* harm us,
if we treat them as things.

The Third Chapter of the Simple Story
(And, it feels like things are now going to get complicated.)

The people of the Sky religion became very comfortable with their words about their belief in a higher power. They set aside special days to go to the temples and pray, and they built bigger and bigger temples. Sometimes they sang about Sky and believed that Sky had sent a special girl child to live among them. Her name was Sunshine. She said she came to show them that they, too, were children of the Sky. She said she loved them and wanted them to be happy and enjoy abundance and love all people everywhere.

They all loved her so much they thought up a new name for their religion. They began to call it the Sunshine religion, and they thought of themselves as Sunshiners.

Life was very good and peaceful for the Sunshiners. Their children began to think that the higher power was Sunshine. They used the word "Sky" and thought that meant Sunshine. Nobody thought to correct that, to make sure they knew what the word "Sky" really represented. Maybe it could not be taught. Maybe they could only find it inside themselves, separate from the words.

Anyway, they were all very sure of their belief and felt very safe with their new religion.

The land of the Sunshine religion ended at the edge of what seemed like an endless stretch of water. The people played along the edge of the water and

eventually learned to swim in the water. One day, a young man had an idea. Maybe he could float on top of the water inside something. He tried several ways of doing that and finally wound up with what we would call a boat. Each day he traveled farther out in his boat than the day before, and one day he took some of his friends and some food. They planned to travel far beyond the sight of their own land.

After several hours in the boat, they sighted land. There were tall buildings on the land which looked like their temples. But as they came closer they saw that it was a different land. The temples looked slightly different. Instead of a sun symbol on the steeples, there were symbols that looked like stars. They also saw people coming down to the shore to greet them, with flowers and food in their hands.

Climbing out of their boat, the Sunshiners greeted the strangers cautiously, but to their surprise they were warmly welcomed. At first it was difficult to understand what the strangers were saying, but soon the Sunshiners understood that the temples were not temples at all. The people said they were "cathedrals" and the Sunshiners thought they meant "castles." The strangers said they went to the cathedrals/castles to talk with the Son of Star, whose name was Starshine. They called themselves "Starshiners"! Slowly, the Sunshiners began to understand that the Starshiners believed that *Stars* were their higher power, that *Starshine* loved them and protected them and forgave them.

This began to alarm the Sunshiners, and they tried to tell the Starshiners that they were wrong, that *Sunshine* was the higher power. But the Starshiners frowned and gestured and looked very troubled. A few

looked angry and began to talk among themselves. All at once, to the utter astonishment of the Sunshiners, they stopped talking and, smiling quietly, they lay flat on their backs with their arms and legs touching, pointing at the sky. They looked like lopsided triangles pointing upward.

This looked so funny to the Sunshiners that they began laughing and pointing. When the Starshiners realized that they were being laughed at, they jumped up, looking and sounding very angry, and began to attack the Sunshiners. They used their fists and the pointed sticks they had been carrying. The Sunshiners, being greatly outnumbered, ran to their boat and escaped.

They sailed back to their island and told their people about the strangers who believed in the wrong god. As they told the story about the attack again and again, they began to believe and add to the story that the

Starshiners' god was *evil*. Then they attached words like "pagan" and "savage" to the Starshiners. As the stories spread, a plan began to form. The Sunshiners would build many boats and get bigger pointed sticks than the Starshiners used. They would sail to the Starshiners' island and attack and capture the people there. They also planned to destroy the Starshiners' "cathedrals" and make them learn about Sky and the Sunshiners' religion.

While they were planning, they taught their children to hate and fear the Starshiners. They didn't know that hate and fear are really the same thing.

And that's where this chapter ends.

This story is starting to feel not so good.

The reason this story doesn't feel good is that we know that people really have been captured and hurt and killed—just because they used the wrong words.

11

If Jesus Christ had been named Elmer, would he still be Jesus Christ?

If your parents had named *you* something else, would you still be *you*? Think for a moment–do you answer to more than one name?

12

How many names does God have?

There is a church librarian named Hazel Gavitt in Escondido, California, who says that there are at least *eleven* names for God in the *Bible* alone. She also says that there are at least *ten* names for Jesus Christ in the New Testament. Elmer isn't one of them, but maybe Mary had never heard of the name Elmer.

Could this be the next lesson, a sort of outrageous idea:

13

Jesus Christ was not a Christian.

Christians were followers of Jesus Christ. He could not have followed himself. But, if he was not a Christian, what was he? Whom did he call on since he could not very well call on himself as something *greater* than himself?

Could this be the end of the primer?

I'm not sure. But while we think about that, let me share this with you.

When I was young and feeling troubled, I used to call on someone whose name seemed to be Waldo. I wanted to feel that there was someone greater than myself or my parents (I had already figured out that they didn't always have the answers), someone who understood things that I did not. Sometimes while I was in school I wrote notes to Waldo. I used to ask Waldo to help me remember what I had studied (or had not studied) for tests.

Often I needed to feel that Waldo was sitting right there with me taking the tests. This seeking of a higher power and writing it notes or simply sharing my thoughts with it ("it" being Waldo, at that age) was something that I just did *naturally.*

All that was before God, called by any name, silently or aloud, was expelled from my school. The way it is, I couldn't even call on Waldo now. Teachers would have to let me know that a higher power exists only in churches, if at all.

And I needed a teacher who would let me know that it was okay if I needed to call on something or someone higher than myself or my teacher. Young kids tend to believe what their teachers say. If their teachers like them, they *trust* their teachers in return and *believe* them. They think they are learning *the* truth. They reason that if a higher power doesn't exist in school, where every fact is known, then it must not exist at all. I wonder how many kids never get a chance even to think about that question. Doesn't it seem that everyone has a right to hear about the *possibility* that a higher power is a *possibility?*

Could it be that leaving out the *possibility* of a higher power in schools is *one* reason why kids and teachers have been feeling more and more troubled in recent years? And, why many keep looking for a higher power in all the wrong places?

While we think about that, let's try to write an appropriate ending to the Simple Story.

The Simple Story – Final Chapter

While the Sunshiners planned their attack on the Starshiners, something wonderful happened.

It seems that the same young Sunshiner man who built the boat for the first trip had recently been making lone voyages back to the world of the Starshiners! Following the disastrous original trip, he made the trip secretly many times. But why?

As the story goes, while he was there the first time, his eyes had met those of a very beautiful young Starshiner girl. He fell in love with her, and she with him. Words and symbols and cathedrals and religions made no difference to them whatsoever. Simply, what was in their hearts was all that mattered. Even though their communication was made mostly by hand signals, looks of the eye, and soft and gentle touching, that was all the language they needed. They knew that they were of the same spirit, and that they were in love.

During the long months of the Sunshiners' preparation for their crusade against the Starshiners, the young couple met often and fell even more deeply in love. In time, the young man secreted the young girl away and they began to live on the remotest part of his land. He called her Star and together they lived an idyllic and simple life. After a while, a young girl child was born to them. Between them, in their own kind of words, a language they had designed, they named her Light. The child Light was called that because the very-much-in-love couple knew that Light itself was the one thing that both of their religions and beliefs had in common.

One day the young man's father, the staunch and sometimes fierce leader of the Sunshiners, came to find the young man. When he did, there was a great anger in his heart at what the young Sunshiner and his Starshiner bride had done. As he loudly expressed his fury, Star quietly listened and watched and understood that the source of his anger was his fear for his son. Understanding this, she bravely approached her new father-in-law and placed the child, Light, in his arms. At first the furious father stiffened with revulsion at holding a child of another race and religion so different from his own. But then, little Light wrapped her tiny hand around his massive thumb and squeezed it gently.

Instantly a vision of his beloved mate, known to the tribe as Wise Woman, came to him, saying, "This is

your grandchild, of your own flesh and blood," and in that moment a tear rolled down the old man's face, following the creases in his leathery skin. The tears came because he knew that this baby, the product of love and harmony between his son and the Starshiner girl, was no different from any other child. How could he go to war and kill his own kind? He knelt before his son and begged his forgiveness. His son got down on his knees and embraced his father with the baby Light between them. And, in that moment, a wondrous event took place that would change the worlds of the Sunshiners and the Starshiners.

The father, a powerful leader who had become a warrior out of fear, was now a grandfather. He slowly rose to his full height and made a solemn vow to both his son and his new family. War in his lifetime against the Starshiners, or any other race that might be discovered,

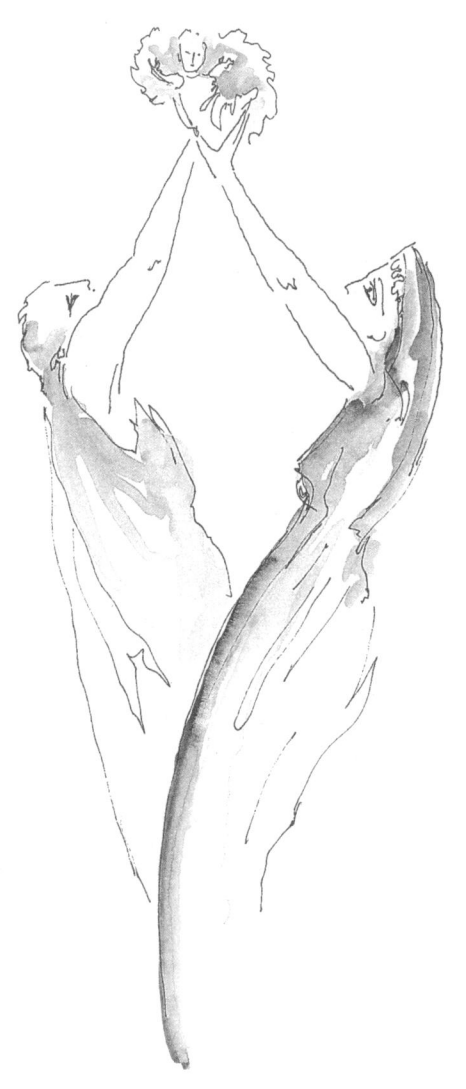

would never happen. He further promised that people could worship trees or water or stand on their heads and pray if they wished. They could call their higher source any of the many names that seemed right for themselves. He would show his people that when they killed or hurt or captured anyone else, they only killed or hurt or captured themselves. And from that day on, he kept his promises. At ceremonies he and Wise Woman held their baby grandchild high for all to see, showing how she proved that all men, all people were the same, no matter where they lived or what they believed.

One day in their waning years, he and his mate were consulting about the future of the tribe. They were thinking about the futures of all the children. They decided to propose a new vision for the tribe, and when they did, everyone enthusiastically agreed. Their vision was that it was every person's birthright to worship whatever and whenever and however he or she chose, and as long as no one else was harmed or hurt by exercising that birthright, no one could interfere.

A second part of the birthright also recognized that *how* a person prayed should never be ridiculed. Prayer was a natural human act, the act of reaching inside or outside one's self for something greater. If you wanted to lie on your back and point your arms and legs at the sky, or if you wished to sit silently and sing a poem to yourself, it mattered not. It was your birthright to do so. And, it was also your birthright to choose not to pray at all.

From that day on, all the people of the land understood that when they looked into the eyes of another, they merely saw their own reflection and that reflection was a reflection of all Life, no matter how it appeared. In time, the people learned that in order to have their freedom, they must be willing to give freedom, and stay connected to all life.

And so it was.

Of course, this is only a possible ending. You might think it is a fantasy or simply wishful thinking. The true ending of the story must be carried out by each of us.

Maybe this could be a wonderful beginning.

If we let it. . . .

And, because it might be unlucky to finish our primer with thirteen lessons, let's add a fourteenth:

14

Everyone together is light,
or, everyone is part of the light.

Epilogue

Actually, the ending must be carried out by you and me and everyone else. But before we get to that, let's make some clarifications about the words we keep using.

Definitions

Prayer in its simplest form is: reaching for a higher source, outside or deep inside oneself, for answers, help, fulfillment, and/or gratitude.

Everyone prays, either consciously or unconsciously. Swearing is often prayer in disguise.

Religion is: a system or set of beliefs about a higher source.

Religious prayer is: using a form of prayer based on and taught from a set of beliefs about a higher source.

Natural Prayer is: a natural human act, reaching outside or deep inside oneself for answers, help, fulfillment, and/or gratitude, *not necessarily* based on dogma, symbols, or religious beliefs.

A Handbook for Taking Action

Here's how we can secure our human right, the right to pray or not pray *as we choose.*

For a few years, I began a multigraded class of 6th, 7th, and 8th-graders, a very hyper age level, with silent reading. The only rules for everyone, including myself, were that we had to have a book open in front of us; we had to at least, look as if we were reading; and we could not disturb others in any way. In the beginning, as expected, a few pupils tested the rules. But in time, everyone was complying by coming into the room eager to "escape" for a few minutes into silent reading. What I looked forward to was the peace and calm that settled over the room and made for easier learning and better cooperation throughout the rest of the period. After our short silent-reading period, all of us–students and teacher–were more "in tune" with one another. The conflicts and challenges outside the door had been laid aside.

A few moments of silence that allowed *natural prayer* would have the same effect and, quite possibly, something even greater. Why not give it a try? Maybe the peace and production the teachers and students create would even carry beyond the schools and into our streets, workplaces, and homes. Sounds too good to be possible? It is certainly a peacemaking thought, isn't it? What could be simpler?

A few moments of *nonmandated silence* including natural prayer is a solution that includes the rights of *everyone,* and is a solution that *everyone* could live with; except perhaps those few who would like each one of us to be exactly like them. There would be immediate benefits; there would be long-term benefits; and it would cost nothing but a very few moments of time.

A simple answer

The ban against prayer in schools was born of the concern that children forced to participate in prayer were having other people's religious convictions pressed upon them. Many felt that was wrong.

So, the question ultimately becomes, "Which religion is the *right* one?"

The answer is, "They all are."

In the end, religions are all about the same thing: a higher source. Each religion is simply a "system," a language, a set of symbols that refer to that religion's God. The bottom line is that each religion is basically about the same thing and is right for the believers of that religion.

The problems arise when one group attempts, forcibly or otherwise, to impress upon any other group its religious beliefs.

When we go to another country and hear a different language, we try earnestly to tolerate and to understand what words express the very same things our language is about. Maybe we need to find a restroom! Languages are about life. And if we are open to the language, maybe we can learn where to find the restroom.

But when we hear a different word than ours for the higher source, we tend to want to convert the speaker–or kill the speaker. *Historically, millions more have been killed than have been converted. And they are still being killed, even in the enlightened almost-twenty-first-century United States.*

An old American Indian prophecy suggests that the Earth is a great cosmic experiment whose purpose is to find out if beings of different races and religions could live together peacefully. And further, since many different peoples have been drawn to the United States, this seems to be the focal point of the experiment. This also suggests that whether you were born in the United States or migrated here, you are a specific part of this experience, and of the mission to show that all peoples can get along together and live in harmony.

So if we want to be part of the solution, instead of part of the problem, where do we begin? Good ideas are only entertainment for our brain until we take action.

Maybe we could begin by looking at religions. You may already have a religion, one which might even be considered agnostic or atheistic. Or maybe you are in the process of choosing a religion, one that feels right for you, suits you, rings bells of recognition in your inner self. Whatever, *go* with those feelings. Enjoy and be enriched by the rituals and symbols and sharing with others. Let that be "natural" for you. And please don't waste your precious time and life-energy making all those other religious languages "wrong"!

Wouldn't it be fun and joyful if we could practice whatever religion we choose without wasting any time making all the others wrong or bad? And wouldn't it be wonderful if we all learned to "Judge not, lest we be judged"?

Nearly all religions have had some "bad" things done in the name of that religion. "Bad" things are always done out of simple greed or fear, and are carried out and perpetuated by members who have forgotten the true basis of their professed religion.

If we accept our simple definition of religion, then atheism could be considered a religion because it is based on a belief about a higher source. The basic tenet: there is no higher source. Atheists get together often and share their language and take actions based on their beliefs. That is their human right, and it is "right" for them.

It does seem unfair, however, that atheism has been the only belief system about a higher source practiced in American public schools for 30 years.

A call for Natural Prayer in public schools: Easy basic and critical guidelines

1. Any leader in charge of any group, whether it be teacher, student, aide, administrator, or other staff member, can choose to allow one or two minutes of silence, stating that it can be used to pray, meditate, daydream, or sleep, expecting group members' respect for each other by keeping the silence. Everyone's rights are included in the use of this time, except the right to interfere in any way with others exercising their rights. Individual rights end where others' rights begin.

2. The leaders may not use this time to teach or suggest any one set of religious beliefs. They may simply acknowledge, if it is not already understood, that it is okay to "pray, meditate, daydream, or sleep!"

3. Natural prayer cannot, by its nature, be mandatory. Therefore it should never be called for over an intercom.

The constitutional amendment addresses religious prayer. "Church" means organized religion. Thus *Natural Prayer* can be considered constitutional. It does not interfere with separation of church and state. It can be allowed in our schools in a way that everyone can endorse, ending the divisiveness. It would cost nothing and take mere moments.

We *can* keep it simple. According to most religions (as well as Albert Einstein), one great intelligent energy is all there is. Everything around us, including us, is simply that energy in different forms, each connected to and affected by the whole.

Here are a few more suggestions that will help get everyone, including the nonbelievers, involved in a positive way, perhaps leading to a solution.

Open conversations with your friends and colleagues. Be brave! It can be fun and enlightening. Some agnostics think that we cannot put the words *natural* and *prayer* together. Why not? You can also start an interesting conversation asking, "Have you heard of natural prayer?" The answer will nearly always be, "What's that?" Answer as simply as you can, and . . .

Listen carefully and openly to the response. Remember, you are not trying to change anyone's belief system. However, you may want to suggest an expanded way to look at their beliefs, adding natural prayer to the possibilities.

It is okay to believe in prayer and it is okay not to believe in prayer. The message in our public schools, for 30 years, has been, "We do not recognize a belief in a higher power or prayer here."

Let's begin recognizing both beliefs.

Well, we have come a long way on this exploration. Should we close with a vision of our mission accomplished?

Hope and harmony are restored. Schools and classrooms are more peaceful, more focused on learning, and more productive than ever before. Our diverse nation finds a common ground of connectedness and moves forward peacefully into solutions for the peace and fulfillment of everyone.

And those hundreds of thousands of children, including the adult ones, faultily programmed by violence, abuse, and family disruption, have found hope to overcome what our society had allowed to evolve through divisiveness and disconnection. Everyone knows we are all in this together, one large crew on this spaceship Earth.

About the Author

Diversity underscores Patty Jo Cornish's background. With experience and recognition as an educator, teacher, author, counselor, management trainer, seminar developer, businessperson, photographer, mother, and grandmother, she simply refers to herself as a peacemaker. She has reached diverse radio, television, keynote and seminar audiences across the country with "Outrageous Ideas," a unique communication strategies program she developed based on psychology and neuro-linguistic programming. That program led to outrageous ideas about prayer and the writing of *The Prayer Primer*. In 1994, with Lynn Sharpe-Underwood and Luann Linquist, she co-founded the Natural Prayer Project in order to create a national conversation and national recognition of Natural Prayer. Patty Jo and members of that Project are available for speaking and leading conversations about the project and "Outrageous Ideas about Prayer."

About the Illustrator

James Hubbell is an artist, poet, sculptor, and designer-builder, known internationally for an intuitive, nature-sensitive approach to his work and life. His greatest volume of commissioned work has been in stained glass, appearing in restaurants (which he also designed), private homes, schools, churches, and a sheik's palace in Abu Dhabi. He has written and illustrated two delightful poetry books. In 1980, the County Board of Supervisors proclaimed a James Hubbell Day in recognition of his artistic contributions to San Diego County, where he resides, calling him ". . . a diversified creative phenomenon, a contemporary Renaissance man living in our eclectic age." Mr. Hubbell and several friends started the Ilan-Lael Foundation in 1982 to promote aesthetic and holistic values in the development of community. He has recently completed an amphitheater in Vladivistok, Russia, in honor of their sister-city relationship with San Diego, and is directing multicultural volunteers in the building of a school in Tijuana, Mexico. He volunteers thousands of hours of his time and talent to create beauty for others.

Acknowledgments
≈

Hundreds, thousands of precious people–my late father and mother; my sisters and brothers; many more wonderful family members, including my sons, Bryan, Tim, Craig, and Tarrell; friends; grandchildren; students; teachers; colleagues; and so on–have contributed to my life and therefore to my contributions, including this book. I thank them all for the lessons they have taught me. And I specifically thank the following precious ones who have contributed immeasurably to the final product:

Several have been giving their support since this work began in 1984.
Lynn Sharpe-Underwood–for constancy and brilliant light
Joel Cornish–for guidance and broad vision
Roberto Quintero–for early editing, magic, and constant prayer
William Galt–for four powerful pivotal points along the way
Herbert Boynton–for unequivocal validation and monumental support
Tarrell Cummings–for the earliest wide-eyed vision of the outcome
Patty Lou Songer–for lasting support and validation
Joyce Thayer–for pizazz and outstanding bravery using
    natural prayer in the classroom
Steve Riller–for unwavering cheering and inspiring energy
Margorie and Ken Blanchard–for inspiration and magical support
Suzanne Couch–for early visions of the possibilities
Patricia Ortlieb–for spiritual reminders along the path

And more angels have arrived recently, each with their special gifts.
Luann Linquist, Ph.D.–for patient coaching and precision editing
George Cossolias–for ceaselessly lending his backbone and brilliance
Robert Cederdahl–for constancy, coaching, patience, and propelling
Bob Arundale–for grinning support and sharing the "Ahas"
Theresa Yuschok, M.D.–for opening her home and heart to the
    first Natural Prayer salon
Linda Kleinschmit–for showing up in perfect time, grace and patience
Erin Garth–for appearing just when her brilliant talents were needed
James Hubbell–for creating the inspired illustrations from a pure heart
Dr. Francesca Bresinhan–for exquisite proofreading and encouragement
Cari Vinci–for ongoing mentoring and walks with Charley
Tessa Cason–for quiet intensity and NPP support
Dolly Goodson–for enthusiasm and being the first Natural Prayer
    Ambassador-at-Large
Marny Leondis–for precious sisterly support and extensive proofreading
Loretta Scott–for unique insights and editing
Jeff Oien–for energy-producing and validating cheerleading
Jerry Messex–for precious start-up support

And, many more angels out there like Mary Elizabeth and Maurgerite. And all the members of the Natural Prayer Project Advisory Board. And all the readers of *The Prayer Primer* who have been out there bravely talking about the ideas and Natural Prayer.

Author's Note
≈

Based upon the ideas in this book, the Natural Prayer Project was co-founded by Lynn Sharpe-Underwood, Luann Linquist Ph.D., and Patty Jo Cornish. The Project's mission is simply to further the understanding and practice of natural prayer.

We believe everyone has had experience with natural prayer and you, especially *you*, whoever you are, are invited to share thoughts, questions, insights, and "yes, buts" about natural prayer.
- Share your *experiences* of natural prayer.
- Share your techniques and experiences of natural prayer in the classroom.
- Initiate conversations and salons to share your learnings.

We may ask permission to publish these in upcoming articles and newsletters.

THE NATURAL PRAYER PROJECT
Box 909285, San Diego, CA 92169
Phone: 800-209-9929 Fax: 619-490-9099

HOW TO ORDER
Please ask your local bookstore owner for copies of *An Outrageous Idea: Natural Prayer.* If it is not yet available, please order at $14.95 per copy from: Hilltop House Publishers, Inc. P.O. Box 909285, San Diego, CA 92169